Conversion Optimization

B. Vincent

Published by RWG Publishing, 2021.

CONVERSION OPTIMIZATION

First edition. June 23, 2021.

Written by B. Vincent.

Also by B. Vincent

Affiliate Marketing
Affiliate Marketing
Affiliate Marketing

Standalone
Affiliate Recruiting
Business Layoffs & Firings
Business and Entrepreneur Guide
Business Remote Workforce
Career Transition
Project Management
Precision Targeting
Professional Development
Strategic Planning
Content Marketing
Imminent List Building
Getting Past GateKeepers
Banner Ads
Bookkeeping

Bridge Pages
Business Acquisition
Business Bogging
Marketing Automation
Better Meetings
Conversion Optimization

Conversion Optimization

Hello, and welcome to this course, conversion optimization. In this course, we're going to cover how to get the most out of your lead pages. This course is divided into three modules. Module One gives you a brief intro to conversion concepts. Module Two covers tools and methods, and module theory covers tweaking and testing. By the time this course is over, you'll know how to optimize your pages for maximum conversions. So, without further ado, let's dive into the first module. Okay, guys, welcome to Module One. In this module, our expert will give you a brief intro to conversion optimization. So, get ready to take some notes. And let's jump right in.

Alright, so let's go over exactly what conversion optimization is. So, on any given page, or in any given advertising or marketing campaign, there's an action that you want your prospects to take. And sometimes it's opting in to an email list or maybe it's getting someone to purchase something from an e-commerce site, sometimes it's entering in a phone number or an address, or it's booking a call or requesting a quote, if it's a sales page, you just want them to scroll down there and get to that Buy button. And sometimes it might be something as simple as a click, whatever the action is, you want as many of your visitors as possible to take that action. And when a visitor takes that action, that is called a conversion, your conversion rate is the percent of visitors that convert, that take that action. So, if you have a landing page with an email, opt in form, and 200 visitors view that page, and 60 of them type in their email address and click Submit, well, there you go, you've got a 30% conversion rate, 60 out of 200.

Now it goes without saying that we want our conversion rate to be as high as possible. A higher conversion rate means that we get more leads, we get more appointments booked, we get more sales calls, more sales, more revenue, and so on and so forth. But there's one word missing from all that. More is good, right? But the missing word is from. We don't just want more of the good stuff. We want more of that stuff, more leads, more sales, more revenue, we want more of it from our existing traffic, or from a given amount or a given instance of traffic coming to our entry points. You see, because you can get more leads and sales by simply spending more money on traffic, by simply sending more visitors to your site, maybe you increase your advertising spending, or you increase your social media prospecting, and you're hustling and all that good stuff. But we don't want to be in a position where that's our only option. We don't want to be in a situation where we're dependent on volume, because we're powerless to change our conversion rates. So, we know that 100 visitors who come to our site, 10% of them are going to buy from us, let's say just for example. And so, oh, well, I guess we'll just have to be content with that. And if we want more sales, well, then we better increase the ad spend and bring more of those hundreds in to our site, so that we get more of those 10s. 10 people out of 100 buy from us. So, let's just get more hundreds so that we get more 10s. I mean, sure that'll work, but it sucks. What we want is to get more sales and conversions out of the existing traffic.

So ultimately, conversion optimization means efficiency. What that does is it drives down the customer acquisition cost, because let's say those 100 visitors that we mentioned cost $100 in ad spend to drive them to our site, and then 10 of them end up buying from us. Well, that means that cost you $10 to acquire a customer. 100 divided by 10 is 10, $10 per customer acquisition. But what happens if you increase your conversion rate from 10% to 20%? So, 20 buyers out of 100 visitors. Well, that means that your customer acquisition cost is now only at $5 because you still spent only that original $100 in ad spend, you didn't change your ad spend but you got twice as many buyers, you got 20 instead of 10. So, 10 divided by 20 is $5 per customer. You've literally Cut your customer acquisition cost in half, which means more profits left over from the sales that you make with those customers. Does that kind of make sense? Conversion rates are not a vanity metric, they're not something that you increase just for the sake of increasing them because they look good or they make you feel good. A lot of people think that way. No, it's actually a very, very significant economic reality. And it can make all the difference in your business. That is why conversion optimization is such a big deal.

Now, I'm not saying that spending more on ads to drive more traffic is a bad thing. It's not, it's a key to scaling. But it's infinitely better to increase ad spend and traffic volume if at the same time, you're getting more out of all of that traffic, by getting a better conversion rate. It's not an 'either or' situation, It's a 'both and' situation. One benefits the other, scaling your ads and traffic benefits from the lower customer acquisition costs that conversion optimization can bring you. Because when your customer acquisition cost is lower, you can easily afford to outspend your competitors and acquire customers at a higher rate than them. So hopefully this was eye opening to you if you hadn't really considered the what and the why of conversion optimization before. But now let's talk about the how, how do we get a higher conversion rate on our lead pages or landing pages or opt in forms? Well, it involves a lot of creativity, and a lot of testing, and tracking, and tweaking, and a lot of playing with cool little tools. And in fact, it's actually pretty fun. A lot of marketers honestly, they get addicted to conversion optimization, because it's just a really cool process to test out all these new things and get creative and see Oh, what happens if we do variation A versus variation B? And then you see the results coming in, either proves, you right or proves you wrong. It's just a really very enjoyable Not to mention a very profitable science. And in the next module, we're going to have a look at some of those tools and methods that I just mentioned.

Hey, folks, welcome to Module Two. In this module, our expert will cover conversion tools and methods. So, get ready to take some notes. And let's jump right in.

Alright, so now we get into the fun stuff, we're going to look at the tools and methods here that you can use to optimize your conversions. Sometimes they work, sometimes they don't, that's the whole purpose of testing. And speaking of testing, the next module after this one is actually going to be even more important than this one, we're doing this one first, because it's a little bit more fun and exciting. People get excited about conversion optimization tools and stuff. And the fundamentals, however, like tweaking your headlines or tweaking your background image, things like that. Those are actually much more important; they'll be covered in the next module. But for this one, we're going to go over cool things like pop ups and bars that slide in and little bubbles that pop up and try to get people to take an action and so on so forth. And so, let's just go down the list here, these are not in any particular order, this is just a list of things that are out there that you can try and that you can apply to your website. Okay, let's start with social proof.

Now social proof can fall into a category where it let's say you have a long form sales page, or even a short form sales page, where you just have a couple of testimonials, a testimonial section with a couple of testimonials or if it's a long form sales page, it would be a lot of testimonials usually, a big section with a bunch of testimonials. Social proof. It's an interesting one because when done in the traditional way with a little testimonial section, it seems really cliche. Most people would agree, it seems cliche, people look at them. And there's always kind of a skepticism about them. But whether they're even real or if they're exaggerated, and so on and so forth. But one of the most important things you can learn and be aware of in the arts of conversion optimization or even in sales and marketing in general is that things that are cliche, even to the customers for some strange reason they often still work. One example is actually pricing. Customers will always roll their eyes and scoff when they see a price at something that ends with 9 or 95 or 97. They hate it. They look at that and they think that you think that they're stupid. They think that you think they don't understand that 9.97 is the same as 10. And they're annoyed by it and yet they're not conscious of this. But it actually still works, it actually increases the percentage. It's been proven time and time again; it actually increases the percentage of people who bought.

So, the very people who are scoffing at it and being, you know, annoyed by it, and who find it cliche and silly, or they themselves are the proof that it actually still works. And so, you'll find that with a lot of these, and one of those areas is social proof. Social proof, sometimes can seem cliche, but when you have a lot of it, boy, it works. It works if you display it in the correct way. So social proof, there's a few different hacks that we can think of here, that you can try out. Number one, more. More, that's a very basic one, there's not a whole lot of science there. You get more testimonials and cram them into your testimonial section. And the cumulative effect of having a bunch of testimonials can increase your conversions. Obviously, as with everything that we're going to mention, this is something that you test because there might be special circumstances that cause them to not have an impact or maybe even have a negative impact. But generally speaking, more would be the first scenario to look at with regard to testimonials and social proof. But another consideration is sort of surgical selectiveness, where instead of having a big old testimonial section where the value is mostly in the cumulative force of how many there are and nobody actually reads any of them, they just see Oh, well, this guy has like 20 testimonials and that influences their buying decision and maybe they're more likely to convert. Instead of doing that, you actually go through and you try to find a small little piece of each testimonial, you're looking for that money quote, the one or two sentence quote and then you do that for each testimonial.

And so, you've got a smaller in terms of size, a smaller testimonial section, but maybe more impactful because people are more likely to read a one or two sentence quote, than they are to read a big old block paragraph in a testimonial section.

So that's another approach to take. Another one, though, is placement. And this is one, this is kind of advanced, and so far as most people don't do this. But there's a lot of value in digging deep into your testimonials, especially if you have a testimonial from a well-recognized person. But even if that's not the case, if you can find one money quote, that's like even a half sentence, even just a half dozen words. Like the phrase worth its weight in gold, or it blew us away or something like that. And you take that quote out and you add a dot to the beginning or the end of it, and put it in quotation marks, and you put it at the top of your sales page or at the very beginning of your sales video. That is surprisingly, very powerful. People see that. And it's one of those less is more situations. It just has kind of an epic oomph to it when people see one of those small short money quotes placed prominently somewhere near the top of your sales page, or the beginning of your sales video if you're doing a sales presentation.

Another form of social proof is actually videos. A lot of people just have a big wall of video testimonials nowadays on their sales pages. And that can certainly be very beneficial and adds a level of realness and believability. And then the final thing is the social proof apps. So, these little bubbles that actually pop up on the bottom left in the bottom right of your sales page or your lead page that say so and so from Idaho, or someone from Franklin, Tennessee or something like that, just joined the program or just bought XYZ product, and they just keep cycling through. So, the bubble pops up, it disappears. And then about a second and a half later, another one pops up with a different person who just bought the product in question. And it's another one of those things that might seem cliche, but in many cases it still works despite being cliche. Because at the end of the day humans are still very much governed by psychology. Though psychological phenomena, whether we think they're silly or not, they are at play and they do work. And the herd mentality is one of those. And so even a person who scoffs when they see those little social proof apps cycling through in the bottom left corner, whether they realize it or not, they are often more likely subconsciously more likely to buy, because they saw that. So that's a useful one.

Another one is chatbots or even one of those chat windows where a real human is either present live in real time or one of those ones where you can type something and maybe at some point in the next, 5, 10, 16 minutes, human will get back to you, so they're kind of pseudo chat windows. Any of those have been proven to increase your conversion rates in many cases. It's not always going to work. But these actually do work. And there's many reasons or many speculated reasons for why even a chatbot that is not human has a positive impact on conversions. Sometimes it's just subconsciously, the fact that there's a window there that someone could type into, maybe it taps into one of those neurological or psychological things inside of us that that makes us feel more comfortable about buying on a sales page. You can debate the reasons, but for whatever reason, they're very effective in many cases for a lot of businesses. In fact, chatbot, according to an article in Forbes, actually brought business owners and increase, a sales increase of 67% from one study that they looked at. And that's pretty impressive as you can imagine. Increasing your sales by 67% is pretty insane for something that is just automated. It's a chatbot, not a human, a chatbot. And so, chatbots are definitely something that you want to consider looking into.

Another one is pop ups and slide ins and bars. So, these are just attention grabbing little features that you can add to your website, you can use a software service like OptinMonster, for example. And you can have these little attention-grabbing things, slide into your website or pop up onto your website. When somebody is on your page, they can be triggered to show up after a certain number of seconds or after they've scrolled down to a certain level or when they're about to exit the web page, it can be exit intent based. And you can convey a lot of different messages, a bar or a pop up or one of those little slides in messages that slides up from the bottom right can convey a bunch of things that can help your conversion rate. You could offer a coupon in those. In fact, coupons are another thing altogether, we'll talk about those in a second. You could have one that pops up and mentions that you have free shipping this week, or something along those lines, you could have one that pops up and brings their attention to a bonus on the page or to a certain feature, or something along those lines. So, your pop ups and bars and slide ends, these little things are more of a channel for presenting conversion optimizing things. So, coupons and bonuses and sales and free shipping offers, those are the things that change conversions, that can affect your conversion rate. And these things like pop ups and attention bars, these are the channels that you can use to convey that to bring people's attention to those things. So those are definitely things that you want to consider investing in, go try a free trial with something like OptinMonster or similar service. Conversion gorilla is a really good one. If you're just interested in the attention bars that slide in from the top or the bottom or push the web page down and present a message, you can stick all sorts of things, you can stick videos in there if you want to. So that's a whole another category of tools that you can use at your disposal to see if you can increase your conversion rates.

We mentioned coupons. Coupons are very powerful. It's another one of those things that people might scoff at sometimes or look at with a sense of skepticism. And yet they still work. They still work. So even something like a 10% coupon on a $10 offer. I mean, what are you saving? Two bucks. for some strange reason that still will increase conversion rates. So, if you can factor in a coupon or a discount code or something along those lines into your offer, that's very often going to be very beneficial to your conversion rates. We also mentioned bonuses, bonuses are great. I mean, adding real and perceived value to an offer is one of the most guaranteed ways to get more people to want to grab the offer. It's very simple science. So, if you have done a good job of coming up with something to offer as a bonus that your target audience will be interested in. And you do a good job of conveying the value, what you feel should be the perceived value, bonuses can go a long way to increasing your conversions. And in many cases, it's going to come down to how do you convey or bring attention to the bonuses.

So, in a webinar, there's a certain science behind the way that you present an introduce the bonuses and go through your bonus stack, towards the end of the webinar, after you've mentioned, the main offer. If you're on a sales page, there's usually a bonus section at the bottom where you can get proactive, and you can actually have pop ups or attention bars that come in, that mentioned that you've just recently added a cool new bonus. And so, bonuses can really help out with your conversion rates. If you can come up with things that are genuinely valuable and seem to your consumers to be disproportionately valuable, that can go a long way, that can really propel your conversion rates even higher.

Another thing is micro commitments. So, the actual type of form that you're using for getting an email opt in or capturing a sale. There's some debate about this. And it's possible that it has changed in effectiveness over the last few years. Just because audiences are seeing more of it, and then they become maybe immune to it or annoyed by it. But there's a case to be made, a strong enough case that it's always worth testing, at least, that if you have an email opt in form, for example, right there on a page, and people can see it, as soon as they get there, they'll be more likely to leave the page because they don't like the idea, it causes some type of micro stress in their brain, having to face the fact that they're going to have to type in their email address. And yet, if you hide that behind the button, just a button that says send me the report, or yes, show it to me or something along those lines, and you have that button there and then when they click it, a light box opens up or some other portion of the form reveals itself. And now they see that they have to type in their email address, they'll be more likely to type it in and hit submit. So that's the argument. And it has been proven many, many times in the past. And it's called micro commitments. Because psychologically, once a person has already clicked the button, this isn't a conscious thing. It's a subconscious thing. Once they've clicked the button, they've already come this far, they've already told themselves that they want the thing that you're offering for free. And if they've told themselves that they want it, well, then they're more likely to then continue on to the next step and click and fill out their email address. So that was proven to be effective. There's no question about that. That was and I'm using the past tense word there, 'was'.

The question now that some people are debating is whether it's still effective, or whether it's one of those things that is sort of lost its effectiveness. Because something similar to the concept of banner blindness, people see it so often, that it has a neutral impact or perhaps even a negative impact if it's annoying to people. So that's why you always test, test, test, even with things that most people would consider fundamental. A lot of people would consider the concept of a two-step opt in form with micro commitments to be fundamental, just one of the basics, but because there's some questioning of it out there, because there's some reasonable and understandable arguments that have been made, that maybe it might be negatively impacting your conversion rates, why not test it, why not run a split test? Which we'll talk about in the next module and see how it works. And that applies really to everything, all these things that we've just mentioned, you always, always, always want to run split tests and try and determine whether or not there's a significant change in conversion rates based on that one isolated variable. And speaking of which, let's go ahead and call an end to this module since we've gone through all the cool little tools and hacks and methods. And let's get to the actual tweaking and split testing stuff, which like I said, really forms the core and then the basics of conversion optimization, and we'll cover that in the next module.

All right, welcome to Module Three. In this module, our experts will cover tweaking and testing. So, get ready to take some notes and let's jump right in.

Alright, now let's look into the testing and tweaking aspect of conversion optimization. This is really the most important and core and fundamental part of conversion optimization. This is where you really got to sort of roll your sleeves up and get into it, change things, see what happens, change things again, see what happens. And the first thing we want to talk about is what to tweak. And there's a long list of things to tweak, anything's tweakable. The idea, though, is that you want to tweak things in isolation, unless you have enough of an ad budget and a big enough volume of traffic that you can do multivariate split testing it, we'll talk about some of the software and the methods for split testing towards the end of this module. But generally speaking, you want to make sure that you do your tweaking and testing in a manner that makes it very clear which one variable made which one difference. Once you're looking at all the data, if you change three things, and you see an increase in sales, or opt ins, well, great, but you don't know which of the three things had that impact. And it's also very possible that one of those three things had a negative impact. So, although you had a net gain, the net gain could have been bigger if it hadn't been for one of those three variables being there. And you won't know what that is or if that's the case, because he didn't isolate the variables. So, variables, very important. We'll talk about that again, towards the end.

First, though, what can you tweak? What can you tweak? The first thing to look at is the headline, the real moneymaker main thing that you're using to capture your prospects attention, and tell them what it is that you're offering them. Depending on the product, depending on the prospects and the target audience and the occasion, you could end up trying to sell a product that you think is super premium quality, or is super premium quality. And you think that's the most important thing to your prospect. And so, you might have a headline that says 100% cashmere wool scarf, only the finest materials. And it does terrible. And so, then you try a different angle. And you say, our best cashmere sweaters 50% off this week only. And that's the headline, that's the big bold font. And that performs way better or maybe it's the other way around, depends on your audience. So, headlines are definitely one of the first things that you want to consider split testing. And that starts with a little bit of brainstorming, you want to make sure that there's a little bit of logic and thinking behind the reason for trying this angle versus that angle. And once you figured out what angle you want to go with, after a little bit of testing there, then you can tweak even further by picking this word versus that word. So, headlines and sub headlines are very important, as are other instances of sales copy. So, I mentioned sub headlines there that that's very important, bullet points are also incredibly important. So, you might find that a bullet point, let's say you're selling a cell phone, and a bullet point that says, Our biggest level of storage yet, 200 gigabytes of storage. Might not do as well if you test that against something that is more benefit driven, rather than feature driven. So instead of that bullet point, let's say that the storage bullet point says, enough storage for all of your favorite songs, TV shows, and special moments or something along those lines, right. So, bullet points, features, things like that are certainly something that you can split test. Sales copy applies to everything, you're guaranteed, the type of guarantee that you have or the sales copy that you use to convey what type of guarantee you have. If it's a digital product that you know that your customers can keep anyway, even if you tell them that they're not allowed to refund it and keep the product. Well, why not just go all the way with it, if you know they're able to keep it anyway, why not tell them that you know what we're so confident that you can request a refund within 30 days, and we'll even let you keep the product.

A lot of people think that that'll encourage abuses, but it's actually quite the opposite, it actually encourages sales. And the amount of revenue that will be at stake because of the small instances of abuses usually is far outweighed by the positive conversion impact that you get, the increased sales that you get from it. So that would be another thing to tweak in the sales copy area. The wording of buttons. This is a very important one. There are psychological aspects at play here that have been shown at least in many different split tests and studies that people like clicking on buttons that say things in the first person as though they are the ones saying them. So instead of download the free report or download your free report, it might say something like give me the report or give me free access Again, things change. And so, something that might have worked two years ago across the board, maybe it doesn't work as well these days. And so, you want to test tweak and test and make sure you're isolating those variables. So, button wording is definitely something to toy around with. And aside from the question of perspective, first person versus third person and so on, and so forth. There are also the words that you use to describe the thing in question or the action. Download might be tested against the word read, read it now versus download it now. Then you might get surprisingly impressive results from one over the other. The name of the product that you're offering, let's say it's a lead page, and you're offering a free report or an E book, you might find that the term eBook and free report, both of those are just so cliche and cringe worthy these days, that calling it a guide or a blueprint, or a game plan, or something along those lines will bring you an increase in conversion rates. So that's another thing that you can certainly tweak and test.

Next, we have shapes, fonts, and colors. So basic things like we were talking about the buy button the moment ago, basically things like the shape of the buy button. And the geometry of the buy button or the opt in button can have a significant impact on conversion rates. In many cases. You know, a rounded button might, for some strange reason, performed better than the rectangular button, or a button that has sort of a 3d sort of pretend light to glare or a shadow to it might just for some reason have that psychological effect of people wanting to click on it because it feels more real. There have been tests that indicate that. You need to do your own tests because not everything works for everybody. And because sometimes things that universally worked change, and they don't work anymore, because audiences change in the psychology of audiences change after they've been seeing things for a long time. But the shape of a button can have a surprising impact. There are a lot of long form sales letter writers who swear by a special design of button that has little dotted or dashed lines and a square around it and certain wording on the inside. And that performed really, really well on old school long form us style sales pages. So, it might be worth using that even if it looks ugly to you. And you'd prefer something a little bit more modern and sleeker looking. Remember, it's about conversion rates. It's about conversion optimization, it's not about aesthetics.

Another thing is, we mentioned fonts, fonts and colors. We'll talk about colors of text and then colors of sort of the more the thematic makeup of your page overall in a second here, let's talk about fonts and colors of text first though, this can be really good, it can also be overused. The best thing to do is isolate and pick out one or two colors that are very contrast against everything else on your page. Usually, it's going to be something like red, bright red. And the very selective about where and when you use it. It might be on the word now in the call to action, where it might be on an important feature or benefit. And the same goes for fonts and styling. So italicizing text in certain areas might have a beneficial impact, making something bold and stand out a little bit more like income claims or an important part of a testimonial, or underlining certain words. These things work in in a few different ways. Number one, they bring attention and add emphasis to specific words, the colors, the bolding, the underlining, and so on and so forth. But they also break up the text and make it easier to read or easier to skim and still understand what you just skimmed. Because most people when they read a long form sales letter, for example, they're just skimming, they're not really reading the entire thing, the vast majority of people. So, if you can increase the amount of comprehension that they have about what you're offering, when they skim by selective and careful use of fonts and styles and colors in your text, that can be definitely very beneficial.

Then there's the question of color overall, like thematically, the color of your background or the top bar on your landing page, or the button or the outline of the opt in box and things like that. You want there to be oftentimes a consistency. And also, an ad sent which refers to not AdSense, the Google thing, ad sent, it refers to a consistency of look and feel from the ad that someone clicked on to come to this page that they're on right now and the page that they've arrived on. So, if you had sort of a blue and white brand thing going on in the ad that they clicked on, try and keep that blue and white brand that theme to the overall landing page and the elements on it on the page that they've just arrived on. It's a psychological continuity kind of thing. And that also applies to background images, background images or any images that you use on the landing page. If someone clicked an ad, if they're looking at an ad for an exercise bike and there's a specific woman on an exercise bike, it can be really beneficial to have that same model. If you're browsing a stock photo website or something, try and get the same model on the landing page or at a minimum, similar lighting and a similar overall aesthetic and thematic look and feel to the ad that they clicked on. So, imagery can be very important.

Imagery and conversions, it goes really deep. Robert Cal Dini has actually in his studies, he's proven that background images can have an incredible and totally subconscious impact on people's decisions and their behavior. So, background images of money might cause someone to buy something or background images, however subtle they are, background images of clouds might make someone more likely to order pillows, I think was one of the studies that he did. It's again, it's one of those things that no one consciously says, oh, I see that in the background. So now I'm going to buy this. It's something that people aren't even consciously aware of. But frankly, it's kind of creepy how effective and how proven this stuff is. So definitely think about your background images. Other feature images especially with regard to people can be really beneficial here, based on the audience that you're targeting. If you're targeting a market that you know consists of a lot of folks in, say, their 60s or 70s in their retirement years, then guess what, having pictures of people in that age group on your landing page, on your sales page, or your OPT in page is going to be really beneficial to you in many cases. If you're selling something in the finance niche, the investment space or financial freedom type stuff, sometimes the imagery of lifestyle stuff, leisure stuff, people on the beach will have a positive impact on your conversion rate. So, these are all things that you really want to test. And, again, you can be very surprised by the results when you test these things.

Pricing is a big one, there's a lot of psychology, behind the numbers in prices. And some of it frankly it's just goofy. It's those facepalm kind of things where you can look at an offer that costed $10 plus $5 shipping, and it had a 10% conversion rate. But then they increase the price to $15. And then they said free shipping, and the conversion rate doubles. I mean, it's absolutely ridiculous that that works. But it does work in many cases. So pricing, like we mentioned previously, sometimes things will be really cliche and corny, like the use of prices that end in nine or 97 or 95. For whatever reason, even though everyone knows that they're Goofy, that it's a silly concept, it still works, it still works really, really well. There are barriers of resistance, psychological resistance that people will be up against when they're considering buying your products. And so, you want to be mindful of that. Okay, your market might have a big barrier of resistance around the three zero mark where they don't want to cross that mark based on the specific product that you're selling, it doesn't have a value that they perceive to be worth $30. When they hear $30, certain things pop into their head. They picture a family meal that they had in their restaurant the other day that was around $30. Or maybe $30 is something that they pay on their utility bill or it's some type of a monthly cost or something like that.

Everyone has psychological ideas in their heads of what certain amounts represent to them. And for a certain product that you're selling, 30 might just be that barrier of resistance. And so as goofy as it sounds, it will very often be worth selling at 27 or 29 instead Logically, it shouldn't make a difference but it does. It does. So pricing is a big deal. Price slashing and demonstrating that you're decreasing the price from what you could charge versus what you are charging, literally slashing, putting a line through number 100. And saying you're getting it for just $67 instead, and so on and so forth. Again, sometimes it comes off as cliche but it does work, it's psychologically proven, it does work. So, you want to toy around with the pricing a little bit, especially if there's variables in your pricing such as shipping, definitely want to consider a toying around with different pricing models and seeing how those impact your conversions. And the list goes on and on. Anything that you see that pops out to you on a sales page or a landing page is something that can be tweaked. And so, the question is, how do you tweak it? How do you tweak it? And it really comes down to software in most cases. You can do it manually; you can send an ad campaign to one page and then the same ad campaign to another page and just make sure they both have the same amount of traffic in the end and then compare how they did. But nowadays, there's so many tools, specifically for split testing that you might as well use them. So split test monkey is a great independent tool. It's independent from any landing page creator that you have.

Basically, you set up the parameters of the split test and it will give you the URLs to use. And there's the entry point URLs and then there's the success point URLs and there's the tracking. And based on your conversions, it'll spit out the results of your split test. Variation B by 25% and then what have you. So split test monkey would be an example of an independent split testing tool.

But most landing page services these days, most of the big ones, actually have split testing built into them. So, they have their own analytics dashboard. And they have their own multivariate in most cases, split testing setup. So, you can go into, let's say, Instapage, for example. And you can create a cool looking landing page, and then there'll be an option to split test and it'll produce more variations of that page. And then each variation, you just tweak one or two different things. And then you will try and tweak only one thing at a time, that's the most effective way to do it. And then, especially if you're working with a limited amount of traffic and a limited ad budget, you really want to be as surgical as possible. But you have these different variations and you run traffic to them. And you can siphon off different percentages of traffic to different pages. Once it looks like you're seeing a winner in one area. And you just look at the results and you make your decisions based on that. If one headline has a really substantial, like a 20 or 30% higher conversion rate than another headline, well, guess what, you better go with that headline or that should be the new standard against which you now test different ideas.

But one thing to keep in mind is going to be numbers and thresholds. The more certain you can be about your results, the better. And obviously, the smaller your sample size, the bigger the margin of error is going to be. So, you don't want a situation where you only sent 100 clicks into a split test, 50 went to variation A, 50 to variation B and you got 20 opt ins from variation A, and you got 10 from variation B. And you're looking at that and you're like, Wow, that's a huge difference. I'm going to go with variation A, sorry, it wasn't a big enough sample group. There are so many factors that could have caused that to come about. And it's very, very possible that if you had had 1000 visitors being siphoned through that split test, you would see very different results. So, you need a large sample group. I would recommend, if you can pull it off, if you have the ad budget for it, I would recommend not making any decisions based on split tests until you have had 100 results, get 100 conversions to look at throughout your split test. So, if that means that you've got to send 600 visitors to your site, and 300 go to variation A and 300 go to variation B and one of them brings in 100 options, that's an approximately 33% conversion rate. Another one only brings in 50. So that's around 15% and change. Well at that point, you can more confidently say, wow, this one has double the conversion rate, this one performs twice as well. Now, even then, even in that case, that's still a pretty small sample group. But you got to work with what you have, or you got to work with the resources that you have. And I would say as a minimum 100 conversions, 100 results would be the threshold that you're really want to try and aim for. The bigger the sample size, the more certain you can be of the results is just the rule to remember there.

So key things to consider here, all variations and all variables that you're trying to test them in isolation. That includes, by the way, what we talked about in the previous module, each of those instances of having, let's say, a pop up with a coupon offer, or having a certain bonus on your page or the social proof bubbles in the bottom left-hand side, those things are independent variables as well. So, you don't want to just slap that on there and have that potentially impacting another split test where you were trying to determine the difference between a headline choice. And little did you realize variation A performs really well. But variation A also had the social proof bubbles in the bottom left, and variation B didn't. And so now, you don't know which of those two things, the headline or the social proof, cause the increased conversions. So, you want to make sure each of these things is tested in isolation or that you are able to track them in isolation with multivariate testing, if you have the software for that. But again, that requires a higher volume of traffic. So, make sure if you're doing multivariate split testing, that you're able to track everything in isolation, and that you have a big enough sample group to draw reasonable and uncertain conclusions from the data that you get out of that.

But that's what it all comes down to, guys, it's split testing. Use a little bit of common sense, use a little bit of outside the box creativity sometimes, tweak things, test things. And just really dig in and enjoy, enjoy the process of increasing your conversion, seeing what it takes to make more from less, more results from less traffic. You're really going to enjoy the decreased customer acquisition costs and the increased profits that you have when you see that a greater percentage of your existing traffic is converting into sales. So hopefully this was useful to you, guys. I hope you get out there, put this stuff to use, put these things into action and start boosting those conversion rates.

Don't miss out!

Visit the website below and you can sign up to receive emails whenever B. Vincent publishes a new book. There's no charge and no obligation.

https://books2read.com/r/B-A-QWUO-IZTPB

BOOKS 2 READ

Connecting independent readers to independent writers.

Also by B. Vincent

Affiliate Marketing
Affiliate Marketing
Affiliate Marketing

Standalone
Affiliate Recruiting
Business Layoffs & Firings
Business and Entrepreneur Guide
Business Remote Workforce
Career Transition
Project Management
Precision Targeting
Professional Development
Strategic Planning
Content Marketing
Imminent List Building
Getting Past GateKeepers
Banner Ads
Bookkeeping

Bridge Pages
Business Acquisition
Business Bogging
Marketing Automation
Better Meetings
Conversion Optimization

About the Publisher

Accepting manuscripts in the most categories. We love to help people get their words available to the world.

Revival Waves of Glory focus is to provide more options to be published. We do traditional paperbacks, hardcovers, audio books and ebooks all over the world. A traditional royalty-based publisher that offers self-publishing options, Revival Waves provides a very author friendly and transparent publishing process, with President Bill Vincent involved in the full process of your book. Send us your manuscript and we will contact you as soon as possible.

Contact: Bill Vincent at rwgpublishing@yahoo.com www.rwgpublishing.com